Talk Life Before You Talk Life Insurance
Achieving Success in Life Insurance Sales

Lester A. Rosen, CLU®

THE AMERICAN COLLEGE PRESS

The American College Press

Copyright ©2014 The American College Press

The American College Press
270 S. Bryn Mawr Avenue
Bryn Mawr, PA 19010
(888) AMERCOL (263-7265)
theamericancollege.edu

ISBN-10: 1-58293-152-6
ISBN-13: 978-1-58293-152-4

Printed in the United States of America

This work has been modestly updated to reflect societal changes.

Publication made possible by Union Central/Ameritas Life Insurance Corp.

The American College

The American College® is an independent, nonprofit, accredited institution founded in 1927 that offers professional certification and graduate-degree distance education to men and women seeking career growth in financial services.

The Solomon S. Huebner School® of The American College administers the Chartered Life Underwriter (CLU®); the Chartered Financial Consultant (ChFC®); the Chartered Advisor for Senior Living (CASL®); the Registered Health Underwriter (RHU®); the Registered Employee Benefits Consultant (REBC®); the Chartered Healthcare Consultant™, the Chartered Leadership Fellow® (CLF®); and the Retirement Income Certified Professional (RICP®) professional designation programs. In addition, The College offers prep programs for the CFP® and CFA® certifications.

The Richard D. Irwin Graduate School® of The American College offers a Master of Science in Financial Services (MSFS) degree, a Master of Science in Management (MSM), a one-year program with an emphasis in leadership, and a PhD in Financial and Retirement Planning. Additionally, it offers the Chartered Advisor in Philanthropy® (CAP®) and several graduate-level certificates that concentrate on specific subject areas.

The American College is accredited by **The Middle States Commission on Higher Education**, 3624 Market Street, Philadelphia, PA 19104 at telephone number 267.284.5000.

The Middle States Commission on Higher Education is a regional accrediting agency recognized by the U.S. of Education and the Commission on Recognition of Postsecondary Accreditation. Middle States accreditation is an expression of confidence in an institution's mission and goals, performance, and resources. It attests that in the judgment of the Commission on Higher Education, based on the results of an internal institutional self-study and an evaluation by a team of outside peer observers assigned by the Commission, an institution is guided by well-defined and appropriate goals; that it has established conditions and procedures under which its goals can be realized; that it is accomplishing them substantially; that it is so organized, staffed, and supported that it can be expected to continue to do so; and that it meets the standards of the Middle States Association. The American College has been accredited since 1978.

The American College does not discriminate on the basis of race, religion, sex, handicap, or national and ethnic origin in its admissions policies, educational programs and activities, or employment policies.

The American College is located at 270 S. Bryn Mawr Avenue, Bryn Mawr, PA 19010. The toll-free number of the Office of Professional Education is (888) 263-7265; the fax number is (610) 526-1465; and the home page address is theamericancollege.edu.

Certified Financial Planner Board of Standards, Inc., owns the certification marks CFP®, CERTIFIED FINANCIAL PLANNER™, and CFP (with flame logo)®, which it awards to individuals who successfully complete initial and ongoing certification requirements.

CONTENTS

The American College iii

Table of Contents v

About the Author vi

Dedication viii

Preface ix

Foreword xii

Introduction xix

Chapter 1: On Mediocrity and Superiority 21
Setting Goals 21
Self-Improvement 22

Chapter 2: The Value of Time 25
A Few Time-Saving Ideas 25

Chapter 3: Forming Habits 27

Chapter 4: Three Characteristics That Successful Agents Have in Common 33
Preparation 33
Confidence 33
Empathy 35

Chapter 5: Organizing Your Values 37

Chapter 6: Attitude 39

Chapter 7: Work 43

Chapter 8: Perseverance 45

Chapter 9: Determination 47

Chapter 10: Leadership 51

About the Author

Lester A. Rosen, CLU®, born November 19, 1912, was a life insurance business legend. He died on December 31, 2006 at age 94. An agent with Union Central Life, he received the two highest awards that the industry bestows on individuals, the John Newton Russell Memorial Award (1975) and the Huebner Gold Medal (1987). He served as president of the Million Dollar Round Table (MDRT), the Life Underwriter Training Council, the National Association of Life Underwriters, the Memphis Life Underwriter Association, the Tennessee State Association of Life Underwriters, and the Memphis chapter of Chartered Life Underwriters. He also served as president, board member, chairman, cochairman, and vice chairman of numerous community organizations.

At the 1966 MDRT Annual Meeting, Lester Rosen delivered a main platform talk in which he discussed his life and his success. The speech was entitled "The Life of the Whole Man." He is undeniably a role model today, several decades later.

After reading this book, one agent said, "I have learned more from reading what Lester wrote than from all of the indoctrinations that my company has given me so far."

I was fortunate to hear Lester speak just once, in 2003, at a Union Central award meeting. He was legally blind and led to the stage by a colleague. There, before hundreds of those whose careers he had lifted, he talked passionately about the *life* in life insurance. He touched yet another generation.

We are proud to share this work with you.

Dr. Larry Barton, CAP®
O. Alfred Granum Professor of Management
President & CEO, The American College
December, 2013

Dedication

Dedicated to Dr. Solomon S. Huebner and Dr. David McCahan, professors of insurance at the Wharton School of the University of Pennsylvania, and the two men responsible for my having gone into the life insurance business.

Preface

I first met Lester Rosen as a fledging agent with Union Central/Ameritas Life Insurance Company. I took an instant liking to Lester and I believe he took an instant liking to me as well. I consider Lester Rosen as my mentor.

Lester's character was defined by warmth, humor, humanity and integrity. His career was defined by the highest level of dedication, passion and honors. He left an indelible impression on all who knew him.

Born in 1912 in New York, Lester was exceptionally bright, entering the Wharton School at age 16, studying under the notable Solomon S. Huebner, founder of The American College. Upon graduation, Lester debated between a $25.00 a week job at the New York Insurance Office and a career in sales. He called Dr. Huebner with his quandary, and recalled this response: *"Rosen, don't take the job. You have learned all the life insurance at Wharton that you need to know. Go out and sell now and get your kicks well you are young."* That conversation launched a legendary career.

Three weeks after that phone call, Lester joined the New York Agency of the Union Central Life Insurance Company. He was recruited by another Hall of Fame member, Charles Bennett Knight. He launched his career in 1929, one month before the stock market crashed. He recalled those grueling early days, "pounding the streets of New York in the depths of the Depression," working days, nights, Saturdays, Sundays, and holidays.

It paid off. In 1934, his first full year in business, he paid for more than a million dollars in business. In 1937, 24-year-old Lester Rosen became the youngest member of the Million Dollar Round Table (MDRT) – a beginning that foretold of many outstanding years to come. His career was temporarily interrupted while he served as a major in the army in World War II, but even that didn't slow him down. He assisted in the sale of National Service Life Insurance to his fellow soldiers.

Lester exemplified this same level of dedication for his 72-year career. He built a devoted clientele in the Memphis area and beyond with his exceptional skill and knowledge, his tremendous persuasive power to motivate people, his commitment to creating the right life insurance strategy for each client, and his attention to detail and follow-up.

For Lester Rosen, success came down to showing respect in the smallest details of his interactions with others. He said, "Form the habits of acknowledging favors, no matter how small; of being on time for appointments; of answering communications promptly; of being thoroughly reliable in what you say and what you promise to do." Integrity defined his business life. His career remains an extraordinary example of devotion to long-term client relationships.

As you read through Lester's 10 concepts on success in life insurance sales, you will soon realize that they are timeless. When Lester received the Huebner Gold Medal on October 5, 1987, he likened it to be the most treasured award of the many he received.

How fitting it is that 25 years later I was awarded the Huebner Gold Medal. Somehow I know that Lester Rosen, my mentor, was with me that day.

Peter C. Browne, LUTCF
Chairman, Foundation Board, The American College

Lester A. Rosen, CLU® was a man who believed in constant improvement. "When you are 'green,' you grow; when you are 'ripe,' you rot," he would say. He sat for and passed his securities exams when in his late eighties – *after* macular degeneration had destroyed his eyesight. He taught us that true "nobility is not being better than someone else; it is being better than your former self." He was a customer on my paper route when I was a boy, my mentor and friend as a man, and – after 41 years in the business – one of the main reasons for my success.

Mr. Rosen's concepts in this book are a quick read, full of clarity and nourishment for your spirit. May you profit from his wisdom!

C. Robert Brown, Sr., CLU®, LUTCF
The UCL Financial Group, LLC
Past President, NAIFA

I first got to know Mr. Rosen in 1987 when I began my career in advanced sales with Union Central Life. Lester asked me for assistance in designing a deferred compensation plan for Dr. Benjamin L. Hooks, the great civil rights leader and Presidential Medal of Freedom recipient, who was then serving as executive director of the NAACP. Lester was an outspoken supporter of the civil rights movement in Memphis in the 1960s and as a result became close friends with Dr. Hooks. He was very pleased with the program Lester and I recommended and I remember to this day my excitement and pride when Lester told me that he had made the sale. From that time on Mr. Rosen and I collaborated on the business, estate, retirement, and charitable giving plans of dozens of families and businesses. Always the needs of the client came first – always the reminder to keep it as simple as possible – always his passionate belief in the power of life insurance to accomplish goals and fulfill dreams. Lester taught me that even in advanced markets – "Talk life first."

John Gephart, J.D., CLU®
Second Vice President, Ameritas Life Insurance Corp.

Foreword

In music, an overture is a musical introduction to an opera. I don't profess that the essays I have written will be as stirring as an opera, but I will open with an overture that will serve to introduce me to you. On October 5, 1987, in Washington, D.C., I was awarded the Huebner Gold Medal from The American College. Following are my words of acceptance on that occasion.

"The year was 1929. In September I matriculated at the Wharton School of Finance and Commerce of the University of Pennsylvania. In October the stock market crashed. In November, my roommate had to quit school to go to work in order to help his father support the family. Men were committing suicide by jumping off bridges and turning on the gas. Bank after bank closed, bankrupting depositors. Insurance companies invoked the contractual right to delay six months in processing cash-value loans. Story has it that a man walked into the home office of one of the giant New York companies and said, "Gentlemen, it is now ten o'clock. I need a $50,000 cash loan by two o'clock. If I don't receive it, you will have a death claim for $250,000 by four o'clock." He got the loan.

That was the climate in which I started my freshman year at age 16. The 18-year-olds considered me a kid, and since they left me alone, I had time to study.

The curriculum in the second year at Wharton included one semester of life insurance as a compulsory course. My quiz room professor was Dr. David McCahan; my lecture professor was Dr. Solomon Huebner. Quiz room class (25 students) met twice a week. Lecture hall (150 students) met once a week.

Dr. Huebner, in his bombastic voice, drummed into us the concept of the human life value of man. The fact that when a man died his income production ceased and life insurance – money delivered at death – took over so that the widow did not have to seek a job or a second marriage to support herself and her children. Yes, life insurance allowed her to continue as a full-time mother. Halfway through the course, Dr. Huebner devoted a full lecture to the financial sacrifices our parents were making to send us to Wharton (at that time, board, lodging, and incidentals came to about $1,600 a year). He emphasized that the investment that had been made in us would be lost in the event of death, and it was our responsibility to set aside a monthly sum from our allowance or earnings to pay a premium on a life insurance policy that named them as beneficiaries to reimburse them for this economic loss.

One of the resourceful sophomores got a part-time job with a life insurance company and immediately started soliciting his classmates. That is how I bought my first policy – for $10,000.

In my third year at Wharton, I had to choose a major subject. I'd taken economics, accounting, business law, real estate, retailing, and insurance. Insurance impressed me more than any of the other subjects, so I decided to take all of the insurance courses the school offered. These included life insurance rate-making, property and casualty insurance, and ocean marine insurance. Since I was impressed with Dr. Huebner, I took another course that he gave on the stock market. I clearly remember some of his words of advice. When a student asked him how to make money in the stock market, he replied, "Buy low, sell high." He said most people buy in a bull market and then sell when stocks decline rather than buying in a bear market and selling when they rise. He also gave us this advice: "When you get out of school, invest $500 in the market and hope that you lose it. It will save you from losing $50,000 later in life."

"Don't let money burn a hole in your pocket," said he. "Accumulate a good cash reserve. In the future there will be other depressions and recessions and when other people have no cash and you do, you can buy stocks, real estate, and businesses at bargain rates."

I graduated in 1933 and stopped by Dr. McCahan's office to bid him goodbye. When he asked me what I was going to do, I told him that I planned to sell life insurance. He said, "Why not take the CLU® exams before you leave Philadelphia?"

I said, "Dr. McCahan, I will probably take them in a few years."

He said, "No you won't. You are going to take them right now. They will be given in two weeks. Review all the sections and take them all at one time. You will never be in a better position to pass the exams because you have had all of the courses from life insurance to economics to sociology to business law and you have just graduated. You will never be better prepared."

Dr. David McCahan

I did as he suggested, and that is how I passed the exams in 1933. I had to accumulate three years of life insurance sales experience before I could finally receive the CLU® designation in 1936.

I returned to my home town of Brooklyn and asked my father what company he thought I should apply to. He said, "I took out a policy for you when you were 16 with the Aetna Life Insurance Company. Why don't you go down to see the general agent, Gilbert Austin." So I did.

Mr. Austin said, "Lester, you are too young (I was 20). Come back when you are 25 and we will do some talking."

I reported this to my father, who then got in touch with a key congressional friend who said, "I have contacts with the New York state Insurance Department. Tell Lester to call me in a few days."

In a few days I called him and I found that I had an appointment with the insurance department's New York City district office. They offered me a job at $25 a week.

Something told me not to take the job right away, but to call Dr. Huebner to see what he thought. On the telephone, I told him of my Aetna experience and of the state insurance department job offer, and asked him if he thought I should take the job. In his booming voice, slamming his fist on his roll-top desk, he said, "Rosen, don't take the job. You have learned all the life insurance at Wharton that you need to know. Go out and sell now and get your kicks well you are young."

I said, "Yes, sir."

My next appointment – on July 1, 1933 – was with the New York City agency of Union Central Life. That same day I was given a contract and a rate book, and I applied for a life insurance agent's license. The training consisted of Monday morning meetings from nine o'clock to ten o'clock, in which I sat with all the other agents listening to sales ideas and product explanations. No financing. No validation.

I learned quickly that although I had a B.S. in economics with a major in insurance and had passed all the CLU® courses, no prospect was interested in that. Here I was a neophyte in the business world; only a month ago I was a lofty senior at the Wharton school. Isn't that the way life is? You are a senior in grammar school and all puffed up, and the next year you are a freshman in high school, starting on the bottom rung. Then you are a proud senior in high school and the next year you are a freshman in college and considered a kid by the upperclassman.

Well, here I was pounding the streets of New York in the depths of the Depression when executive secretaries were earning $35 a week and insurance companies were advertising: "Buy a retirement income policy so that you can retire at age 65 with $250 a month." I was fortified with insurance knowledge but lacking in practical experience. I worked days, nights, Saturdays, Sundays, holidays – it made no difference.

I talked life before I talked life insurance. I remembered Dr. Huebner teaching that life insurance is money delivered in the future, paid for in the present on the installment plan; that there is no substitute for life insurance, which creates future wealth at the stroke of a pen; that the cash value of a policy is prime collateral because you can pledge it at the bank and get a loan at 2 percent interest.

Gradually, I got into the business insurance market and talked about key-man indemnity plans, stock retirement plans, and partnership buyouts.

I always talked life before talking life insurance and I recognized that there is no substitute for the life insurance contract. I never wanted to be known as a highly technically qualified life insurance man. I was complimented when a client said, "Lester is a good life insurance man." He meant that I understood life, that I understood what he should be accomplishing, and that he recognized that he could place complete confidence in me and feel comfortable with me as a person.

Yes, Dr. Huebner motivated skeptical college students, not by dissecting the life insurance product and saying it is a good buy, but by talking about life and pointing out clearly how life insurance can satisfy a crying need. Yes, a good life insurance agent emphasizes high-touch more then high-tech qualities.

In 1927, Dr. Huebner founded The American College. It was his long-burning concept that life insurance is a professional calling. In the life insurance business world, no academician was held in higher regard than Dr. Huebner. Life insurance companies that he contacted, as well as the Wharton School, supported the establishment of The American College and its ultimate award — the Chartered Life Underwriter (CLU®) designation.

That was in 1927. Dr. Huebner was founder of The American College. Dr. David McCahan was its first president. Both of these outstanding men were my professors. What a rich heritage I have.

Dr. Huebner, I hope you are listening in heaven when I say that – 55 years after I sat at your feet as a student, exposed to your life insurance lectures and having served as a member of the board of trustees of the college that you founded – I now toast you and thank you for giving me the foundation for a successful life insurance career. Not in the state insurance department. Not in the home office of a life insurance company. But as an agent selling money for future delivery and adding tens upon tens of millions of dollars for the benefit of families, individuals, and businesses.

Dr. Solomon Huebner

I'm not sure what I have done through the years to prompt the selection committee to grant me this honor today, but I am grateful to them. I shall cherish the medal awarded to me, Dr. Huebner, which bears your name, and shall place it in my office directly under the personally autographed picture that you gave me in 1954. And lastly, Dr. Huebner, thank you for saying to me, "Rosen, go out and sell and get your kicks while you are young."

Note

I have credited my sources of information whenever possible. However, some of what I've written here I read long ago and have repeated countless times over the years. Unfortunately, in some cases, I have either forgotten or lost the original source.

I extend both my sincere thanks and an apology to these long-lost sources. They have enriched my life and my career, and I regret my inability to cite them here.

Introduction

Ten Pennies are Better than One Dime

Grandpa asked his five-year-old grandson, "What would you rather have, 10 pennies or one dime?"

After a moment's thought, the grandson said, "10 pennies."

"Why?" asked Grandpa.

"Because if I lost one, I would still have nine left."

And so let us look at 10 concepts I've garnered over 57 years of life insurance selling experience. If you don't like one, you will still have nine others. If you don't like nine, you will still have one.

1.

On Mediocrity and Superiority

Determine that you will work hard. Doctors say that hard work has never killed anybody, yet they know of instances when hard work has scared people half-to-death. A man once said that a hard job is the only kind of job he wants because there is so little competition at that level.

Some people have determined that they will be satisfied with mediocrity. Mediocrity is attained by chance. Superiority is attained by design. Do not be content, however, with being average. Being average means either being the best of the lousiest, or the lousiest of the best. Yet there is no nobility in being superior to some other person. True nobility is being superior to your previous self.

SETTING GOALS

I have never had to set production goals. I never stated that I would write so many cases a year or produce so much volume, because these things came naturally from hard work. The only goal that I ever had was to work diligently all day, every day. I did not waste time. I did not take an hour and a half for lunch. I did not take coffee breaks. I put in a full days work, and a full evening's work if necessary. I worked during the heat of the summer, the cold of the winter, Saturdays, Sundays, and holidays – it didn't make any difference because there were always people on whom I could call. And I have consistently written over 100 cases per year.

I don't necessarily advise that people entering the insurance business today not set production goals. However, instead of establishing a volume goal, I do recommend establishing a number-of-cases goal. If you set a goal of 100 cases a year and then perform the level of work necessary to accomplish that goal, I will absolutely guarantee your success.

SELF-IMPROVEMENT

Think in terms of "What can I do to better myself?"

Since how you speak is so important, a public speaking course is one self-improvement step that every agent should take. It will give you great confidence and prepare you to make a convincing presentation to a prospect, the prospect's attorney or accountant, or to a board of directors. Many cities have Toastmasters Club, which usually meets monthly. Members prepare a five-minute talk on any subject they choose, and during the monthly meeting each is called on to give an impromptu talk for two minutes on a subject that is not assigned until he or she is standing before the audience. After the presentation, fellow members critique the speaker. The critique is based not so much on how the speaker developed the subject, but on the authority in his or her voice, gestures, mannerisms, and articulation.

Does this develop confidence? I should say so! Words can always come if thoughts precede them and fear does not chase them away.

I vividly remember an incident as a member of the Toastmasters Club in New York City shortly after graduating from college. A man was called on and, as he faced the class, his knees trembled and his voice cracked. Nevertheless, he made it through the two minutes, after which he received tremendous applause. After six sessions that same man developed into one of the clearest thinkers and most dynamic speakers in the group.

After my involvement with the Toastmasters Club I attended a monthly adult education course at Columbia University entitled "The Body in Acting." This course was extremely valuable to me. It taught me facial gestures, hand gestures, how to walk, how to sit, how to get up from a chair – all things that are very important when you are in front of a prospect or with people in general. I was the only one in the course who did not have aspirations to become an actor. (But I missed an opportunity – I did not get all the other students' names as prospects!)

Another thing I did years ago was to enroll in the Executive Leadership Institute at Southwestern College (now Rhodes College) in Memphis, Tennessee. Southwestern picked up the concept for the course (which was funded by the Ford Foundation) from one that had been developed at the University of Pennsylvania when the president of Pennsylvania Bell Telephone (a Wharton School graduate) observed that his junior business executives were well-schooled in business but were lacking in the humanities. He suggested that if the University of Pennsylvania developed a specialized course, he would send his executives at Pennsylvania Bell's expense. This Penn did.

The Executive Leadership Institute class met one morning per week for two years. Of about 35 in the class, I was the only one who paid his own freight – the others were corporate employees and executives. The class exposed us to the best brains in the country in the humanities – architecture, sociology, philosophy, and so on.

The class in the executive leadership absolutely enabled me to be a better life insurance salesperson – because *you cannot talk life insurance before you talk life*. A conversation about life insurance develops naturally once you sit down with a husband and wife or with a business executive and talk about life. In a sense, this helps establish your reputation and your credibility.

Thanks to the self-development I've undertaken, I have at no time ever felt hesitant about meeting people and talking to them about life and life insurance.

Such self-confidence can be developed. One doesn't have to be born with it. In high school (I started young at age 12 and graduated at age 16) I was not active in anything. I was a good student, and I graduated in the top quarter of my class, but I was not active – not president or head of anything, not even a rah-rah boy – nothing to cause anyone to say, "Well, there's no question that this guy will be a success when he gets out of school." I showed no inclination nor aptitude for anything that at time other than just being a decent kid. Not until I graduated from college (at age 20) did I decide I would step out and prove myself by taking these various courses. The result was that I became active in many things in the insurance business and in the community.

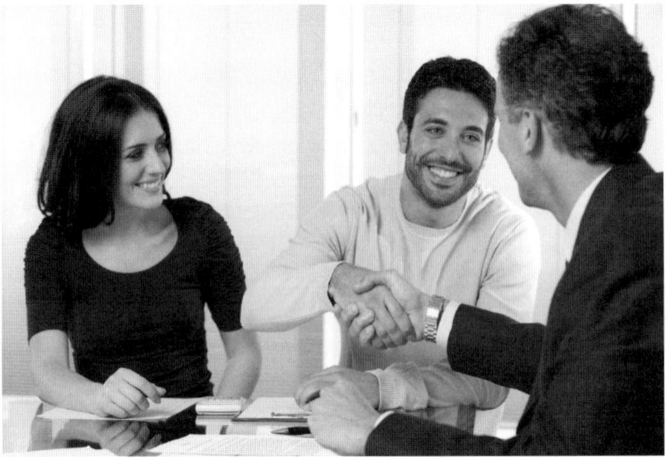

2.

The Value of Time

Time is the inexplicable raw material of everything. With it all is possible. Without it, nothing is possible!

You wake up in the morning, and lo! Your purse is magically filled with 24 hours of time. It is yours. Time is the most precious of possessions. No one can take it from you. It cannot be stolen. No one receives either more or less time than you receive.

In the realm of time, there is no aristocracy of wealth nor of intellect. Genius is never rewarded by even one extra hour a day. And there is no punishment – waste your infinitely precious commodity as much as you will, and the future supply will never be withheld from you. You can only waste a passing moment. You cannot waste tomorrow – it is kept for you.

It has been pointed out that a plain bar of iron is worth five dollars. This same bar of iron is worth $10.50 when made into horseshoes. If made into needles it is worth $335. If made into pen knife blades, it is worth $3,285. And if turned into balance springs for watches, that identical bar of iron is worth $250,000.

The same is true of time. Some life insurance agents can turn an hour into horseshoes, while others can turn it into needles. A smaller number know how to change it into knife blades. Only a few have learned how to transform a golden hour into true-tempered watch springs.

A FEW TIME-SAVING IDEAS

Confirm all appointments by telephone or text message. If a number of days has expired since you made an appointment, call the suspect, prospect, or client (or his or her assistant) and state that you are confirming the appointment and that you are looking forward to meeting him or her at the designated time. This confirmation helps you avoid the possibility that the person may be out of town, has forgotten completely, or is so busy that another scheduled time would be more appropriate. Confirming will prevent *no-shows*. You won't waste time traveling. You'll also impress on your prospect or client that you are a businessperson. Don't fret if by calling you find out that the prospect or client has changed his or her mind and doesn't want to see you – you will have saved yourself a 98% chance of complete disappointment.

Use a pick-up service. If you are in a hurry to receive medical forms or other important papers, and the source is a good distance from your office, do not take the time to pick them up yourself. This could be a wasteful, nonproductive use of time. Call a taxicab or mobile delivery service. The charges are nominal – and certainly less than the value of your time. Certainly, if you only need a copy of a document, use a fax machine.

Have an assistant. As soon as possible, share the service of a talented assistant with one or two other agents, and as soon as you can afford it, enlist the services of a full-time assistant. The assistant's job is to perform various forms of client contact, including service work, sending birthday cards, etc., in addition to any bookkeeping that must be done. You have to release yourself for prospecting, interviewing, and closing. This support person manufacturers time for you to accomplish what only you can do.

My assistant of 35 years, Geneva Whaley, handled about 85% of the phone calls that come into my office, so I usually didn't even become involved. At some time, usually over lunch, she reported to me on the phone calls and lets me know about any prospective situations. Because there's scarcely a technical question that she can't answer, it wasn't unusual for me to come to her with questions.

At my age, I've been asked whether I ever thought of retiring. My answer is always no. Why should I retire when I enjoy what I'm doing? As long as Geneva continues to work, I will work, too. I depend on her so much that in business situations I don't use the pronoun *I*, I use the pronoun *we*. If she ever quits, I'd be hard pressed to determine what to do in the future.

Keep a double-page calendar. One page should have space for you to annotate your appointments; the other page should have space to list telephone calls and things to do. Underscore in red those things that are necessary to accomplish that particular day.

3.

Forming Habits

From time immemorial, men have sought shortcuts to wealth, eternal youth, and success. During the Middle Ages, alchemists sought the elixir that would transmute base metals into gold. They were unsuccessful. Early North American explorers searched for the Fountain of Youth. They, too, were unsuccessful. Now, in our own time, mankind searches for a common denominator for success.

Unlike the fruitless search for a magic formula for wealth and youth, I believe that there *is* a magic formula for success. It was expressed years ago this way: "The secret of every person who has ever been successful is that he or she formed the habit of doing what failures refuse to do."

A habit starts with a change that is too slight to be noticed until it becomes too strong to be broken. What habits can be formed?

Form the habit of refusing to take a 15-minute break every morning and a 15-minute break every afternoon. The only person who ever needs a break is the one who works so hard that he or she doesn't find time to take one. The 15-minute break has not always been with us. It started during World War II in assembly plants to break up the monotony of doing routine work. Today, the break has deteriorated to the point where it breaks up the monotony of doing no work.

Form the habit of going to lunch with someone other than fellow agents. Agents will not buy insurance from you, nor will they suggest prospects. Instead, invite to lunch attorneys, accountants, and others who are in key positions – not for the purposes of conducting an interview, but just to share ideas. You'll be surprised at the subjects for conversation you can generate that can lead to profitable situations. Ask an attorney a leading question, such as, "What was the most interesting case you had in the last two months?" You could reciprocate by reciting or manufacturing a case of your own that you feel would stimulate the attorney's interest, either for himself or herself or for a client.

When I first came into the business and for years afterwards, I always tried to eat lunch with young friends of mine – college friends, club friends, attorneys, accountants, architects, friends starting their own businesses, and so on. I'd make an appointment to have lunch to expose myself to somebody who might be in a position to share valuable information, which could be a prospective lead. "By the way," he might say, "it just occurred to me that you might want to call on so and so who's a friend of mine and who just had a baby..."

Form the habit of prospecting intelligently every day. "No prospects, no sales, no career," stated insurance reporter Carole King, in a *National Underwriter* article. Where can we find qualified prospects – qualified from the standpoint of ability to pay premiums?

- Web, LinkedIn, business association and other lists
- Executive profiles in many daily newspapers and web sites
- New business firms and new partnerships that are created by doctors, accountants, and lawyers
- Personal observation
- Members of your church or synagogue
- Fathers and mothers of young clients who are executives and/or business owners

I have one criterion for prospecting: I only prospect among people who I am fairly sure have money. They aren't necessarily entrepreneurs or professional people, but salaried people who earn enough to pay premiums. Prospecting in such a market is better than performing an analysis of a prospect's needs, only to find out the prospect doesn't have enough money to pay the premiums. Therefore, I telephone everybody who comes to my attention who I feel has the ability to pay premiums.

When I started in 1933, during the depths of the Depression, I was fortunate because my two older sisters married men who were in business for themselves, as was my father; therefore, I was able to naturally contact people who were in the same business and those with whom they did business. Those were the prospects I started with, and from that point I used the so-called "endless chain" system I soon got into the business insurance field.

Widows have needs. I have placed millions of dollars in single-deposit deferred annuities since 1982, about 70 percent of which has been placed for widows. A widow usually has more money than she ever had as a wife. When I started, if a person had $100,000 of life insurance, that was a big deal. Today, a quarter of a million, half a million, or a million dollars is not unusual in the market I working.

I believe that life insurance agents who don't cultivate widows are missing a tremendous market. Widows often come into a great deal of money, then walk into a stockbrokerage office knowing no one in that office and ask to talk to someone about investing money – usually money created by a life insurance agent. Many agents who have been in the business a long time and who have established a reputation in the community overlook this lucrative market.

She can be the widow of a client or one who comes to the agent's attention through church, social, or newspaper sources. What a wonderfully satisfying experience to have widows purchase two to five additional annuities throughout the year and thank you for your counseling. I can name a number of widows whose money has more than doubled since the initial deposit.

Form the habit of contacting prospects in a low-key, straightforward, businesslike manner. When you call someone whom you read about in the newspaper, open by saying," Mr. Jones, let me introduce myself and tell you why I am calling. I am John Smith of the Ajax Life Insurance Company. I read about (the item in the newspaper), and I wish to mention to you that I consider myself as qualified (if you are relatively new in the business, substitute 'we consider ourselves as qualified') in life insurance as you are in the (type of) business. I would like to meet with you one day this week for no more than 20 minutes. I may be in a position to give you some helpful suggestions about life insurance/estate planning and income continuation in the event of disability. Whether we do business together next week, next month, or next year is not as important, Mr. Jones, as just getting to know you. Would you be so kind as to look at your schedule and let me know if I can come by and visit with you briefly on Thursday or Friday morning?"

End your presentation with silence and wait for the prospects answer.

Condition yourself to believe that you have the right to call anyone but that not everyone will do business with you. Any time a prospect interrupts, stop and listen. You learn much more from listening than from talking.

At your first appointment, if Mr. Jones is a stranger, after greeting and allowing him to talk, open with, "Mr. Jones, I know little about you, and you know nothing about me. Please let me take a few minutes to tell you something about myself."

Briefly discuss your educational background, business experience before life insurance (if it is meaningful), your years in the insurance business, and the attainments of your associates indicating that your agency is a functional specialist in every field of insurance. If, at any time, Mr. Jones interrupts, keep quiet and listen.

Continue with, "Mr. Jones, I have no preconceived ideas of what plans you have made, nor of how much life insurance you may have. May I ask you a question? If you died yesterday, what would be the position of your family (or your business) today?

Remain quiet and wait for a response. You are now on the road toward your destination.

Form the habit of contacting <u>today</u> any likely suspects or prospects that come to your attention. Tomorrow someone else may sell them the policy that you could have sold.

Don't neglect your friends. The story goes that Henry Ford purchased such a large amount of life insurance that it made headlines in the Detroit newspapers. A close friend of Ford's – a life insurance agent – literally stormed into Ford's office and asked, "How is it that I did not get the business?" Replied Ford, "You did not ask for it." The friend assumed that when Ford was ready to buy life insurance he would call him. Ford assumed that the friend was not interested. And when we assume – like the spelling of the word – we make an "ass" of "u" and "me."

A psychology consultant to the Louisiana State University School of Marketing had four children but had no insurance, because no insurance agent called on him.

It is reported that a U.S. President, before his presidency, was appointed to the board of directors of an eastern life insurance company: he had $10,000 of life insurance at the time.

Supreme Court Associate Justice Felix Frankfurter had $10,000 of life insurance when he died.

We assume that prominent people in the community are well insured and well advised. Not necessarily so. Call these people. We assume that relatives of prominent life insurance agents are also their clients. Not necessarily so. They may not even be talking to each other! Call on them!

In New York City in the 1930s, I presented an insurance idea to a young attorney whose father was in the insurance business. He said, "Lester, that's very interesting. You know my father's a life insurance agent, but because you've presented this to me, I'm going to buy from you."

Form the habit of exercising daily. A strong body contributes to an alert mind. Build up your circulatory system, exercise your heart and blood vessels, swim, walk, jog, or jump rope.

I exercise regularly. I perform stretch exercises every morning for 15 to 20 minutes, as religiously as I brush my teeth. I swim about a quarter of a mile two to three times a week. I also play golf, although I don't consider golf exercise. I used to do headstands regularly but I cut that out because I'm afraid my body just isn't as supple as it used to be.

Form the habit of working eight hours a day, 10 hours a day, or 12 hours a day, if necessary. If you think you are working too hard, consider the surgeon who is in the operating room at 7:30 a.m. and makes rounds at 6 p.m., or the taxi driver whose shift, day or night, is usually 12 hours.

Form the habits of acknowledging favors, no matter how small; of being on time for appointments; of answering communications promptly; of being thoroughly reliable in what you say and what you promise to do. If anyone writes me a note or letter complementing me for something, I'll promptly drop him or her a one-liner thanking them for their thoughtfulness. (How many people do not respond to letters? I find it perplexing that so many people never even bother to acknowledge a letter of praise.) If I'm running five minutes late, I call and let the client or prospect know I'll be late. Anyone who calls me gets a prompt answer irrespective of who it may be. We can be working on a substantial case, but if a client who has a small amount of insurance calls with a question, Geneva or I answer it promptly.

Above all, do not promise to form a habit and less you have formed the habit of keeping your promises. The weaker your work fiber becomes, the less chance you have of building it back up again. Don't weaken it by making insincere promises.

It is standard operating procedure for us (Geneva and me) to do what we say we are going to do. If we say we'll try to get an answer to a client by the afternoon but aren't able to do that, we'll call back to explain that it's going to take a little longer. That's the way we operate.

When you keep promises, you build trust. I have presented ideas to clients and have had them sign all of the papers on the spot, saying, "Lester, you know I don't sign papers without reading them for many people, but I do for you."

Good habits are your best servant. Bad habits are your worst master.

4.

Three Characteristics That Successful Agents Have in Common

What do successful agents have in common?

PREPARATION

A prerequisite in medicine, law, and the ministry is preparation. Can you imagine a surgeon not preparing for an operation? A lawyer not preparing a case before facing a jury? A minister not preparing for a Sunday morning sermon? Prepare, prepare, prepare – rehearse, rehearse, rehearse.

In one of his poems, T.S. Eliot wrote, "The end precedes the beginning." A football game could not be played if the goalposts were not evident. A foot race could not be run if the finish line was not known. It will avail nothing for an agent to read a hundred books and listen to a hundred lectures unless the end to be accomplished precedes the beginning. It is not the copious notes you take, but what you do with them that counts. Ideas only work if you do.

Have a goal in mind for every call you make. I know what I want to accomplish every time I make a call on a prospect or policyholder. I always prepare in advance what I'm going to say. Am I simply seeking to establish a relationship? Am I aiming for a sale and an application? As I drive to the call, I don't listen to the radio; I concentrate on what I'm going to say, and I review in my mind the responses I might get from a prospect and how I will answer them. I do not wish to be startled by unexpected responses.

CONFIDENCE

The late Dr. Maxwell Maltz, a successful plastic surgeon, wrote the best seller *Psycho-Cybernetics*, which means "steering your mind toward a productive goal." Maltz wrote, "Man has made many discoveries, but if you discover the vast space of mind, you will discover the most important treasurer of all – yourself! Socrates said it in two words: "Know thyself." Only one half of one percent of people have disfigurement of face from accident or deformity, but 90 percent of normal people have an inner scar from frustrations and failures. You must be your own plastic surgeon to remove these scars, and your success mechanism will work for you. When you have negative feelings, when you are concerned with mistakes of yesterday, bring out the confidence of past deeds. . . You cannot be a friend to others unless you are a friend to yourself. You can not respect another until you respect yourself."

It therefore follows that you cannot instill confidence in others until you have confidence in yourself. You must be positive in your attitude and speech. Remember, you are not talking about life insurance, but about money delivered in the future purchased today on the installment plan.

Maltz put it this way: "Chances are that you won't even entertain the idea of going into business unless you have a certain amount of confidence in yourself. But there's a big difference between a false confidence that evaporates easily, and the quiet confidence based on some real accomplishment in the past.

When you step into a doctor's office, and the doctor shakes his or her head, tells you that you must follow a certain regimen, and then writes out a prescription in a language that you don't understand, which is filled by a druggist, in a bottle, the contents of which you don't know – you accept all this because you have confidence in the doctor. And you have confidence in the doctor because the doctor has confidence in himself. The doctor has confidence in himself because he has had training, practical experience, and has made correct diagnoses.

When a man goes to a lawyer to have an estate plan and a will drafted for a million-dollar estate, and the lawyer presents him with an 18 page document that includes a marital deduction trust, a residuary trust, a sprinkling clause, and provides for powers of investment of the trustee, the man quizzically asks the lawyer, "Are you satisfied with this? Is this what I want?"

And the lawyer says, "Yes, it is."

The man says, "Where do I sign?" And he signs because he has confidence in the lawyer, and he has confidence in the lawyer because the lawyer has confidence in himself. The lawyer has confidence in himself because he's had the training and the practical experience, and he has probated wills that have accomplished their purpose.

When you talk *life* before talking life insurance, the prospect asks, "Is this the right plan for me?" You answer confidently, "Yes, it is." The prospect signs because he has confidence in you. And you have confidence in yourself because you have settled death claims, the proceeds of which you helped create.

The doctor who does not have confidence of the public is known as a "pill pusher," the lawyer who does not have the confidence of the public is known as an "ambulance chaser," and the life insurance agent who does not have the confidence of the public is known as a "policy peddler."

EMPATHY

Empathy is the ability to put yourself in another person's shoes, to tune in on the same wavelength. This is how you establish rapport with prospects.

Advisor Paul Rothkrug, answering the question, "How do you reach a prospect?" said, "You don't reach him with an artful presentation. You don't reach him with a complicated illustration. You don't reach him with a tax gimmick. You don't reach him with a clever argument. You reach him through the chemical interaction of your two personalities. Compassion… The ability to feel with and for someone… the ability to make his problems your own… to respond to them in the same intense personal way that you respond to your own problems… to subordinate your interests to his needs… and, above all, the ability to project it so that he feels it, too. Deep inside of you, because you are a human being, is that most human quality: *compassion*. Bring it out… develop it. Above all, trust it!

Trust yourself to show it… And your clients will trust you with their very lives."

People buy, not because of what they think they need, but because of what you think they need. The greatest compliment you can receive is when a client thinks you after signing an application or after you deliver a policy. Do not respond, "Thank you for your business"; rather say, "Thank you for giving me the opportunity to be of service to you. I value your confidence and friendship."

5.

Organizing Your Values

Professor Hugh Russell of Georgia State University said:

> "Perhaps the most frequent thing said by men about success is, 'if only I could become better organized I know I would be more successful.' But being well organized certainly does not guarantee success. We all know individuals who have a most efficient filing system, who have cross-indexed prospect cards and elaborate calendars and timetables so that every minute of their day is accounted for and utilized, and yet we frequently see that these same people are not achieving success in any area of their lives. Something is missing! In short, the successful man has found a way of organizing his values. He has learned to differentiate quickly between the important and the unimportant; to know his priorities. During every minute of his working day he is either consciously or unconsciously selecting those things that are of most importance and making sure they are done even though things which have lesser importance might go undone."

In this short paragraph, Dr. Russell has given the recipe for the attainment of success in both one's business and one's personal life.

I know my priorities. I know that prospecting is the most important aspect of our business – no prospects, no sales. If you are new to the business and don't have , then do your filing, birthday cards, etc., on Saturdays, Sundays if necessary, or evenings when you don't have appointments. This relieves your prime-time hours for prospecting and sales.

6.

Attitude

Perhaps you are familiar with the hotdog story:

> A man lived by the side of the road and sold hot dogs. He was hard of hearing and so he had no radio. He had trouble with his eyes so he read no newspapers. But he sold good hot dogs. He put a sign on the highway telling how good they were. He stood by the side of the road and cried, "Buy a hot dog, mister?" And people bought. He increased his meat and bun orders. He bought a bigger stove to take care of his trade. He brought his son home from college to help him.
>
> But then something happened. His son said, "Father, haven't you been listening to the radio? We have double-digit inflation. The Middle East situation is terrible. The domestic situation is worse." Whereupon the father thought, "Well, my son has been to college. He reads the papers and he listens to the radio, and he ought to know." So the father cut down on his meat and bun orders, took down his advertising signs, and no longer bothered to stand on the highway to sell hot dogs. And his hot dog sales fell almost overnight.
>
> "You're right, son," the father said to the boy. "We are certainly in the middle of a great depression."

It has been said that your attitude, not your aptitude, determines your altitude in life. Sales can be made during a depression or recession, during a blizzard or a heat wave, during a flood or a drought, during summer vacations or the Christmas holidays.

During the depths of the Great Depression in the 1930s, people were not buying Schrafft's Candies, but they were buying nickel Hershey bars; they were not shopping at Saks Fifth Avenue, but they were shopping at Woolworths 5 and 10. Somebody was working. Somebody was making money.

A story goes that one night in ancient times three horsemen were riding across the desert. As they crossed the dry bed of a river, out of the darkness a voice called "Halt!" They obeyed. The voice told them to dismount, pick up a handful of pebbles, put the pebbles in their pockets, and remount. Then the voice said, "You have done as I commanded. Tomorrow at sunup you will be glad and sorry." Mystified, the horsemen rode on. When the sun rose, the horsemen reached into their pockets and found that a miracle had happened. The pebbles had been transformed into diamonds, rubies, and other precious stones. They remembered the prophecy. They were both glad and sorry – glad they had taken some and sorry they had not taken more.

This is the story of life insurance! A widow was glad that her husband had taken some insurance and sorry he had not taken more. A man is sorry that he did not buy more insurance when he was younger, because now he is uninsurable.

We have to be as commanding as the voice that called "Halt!" *Ours* must be the voice to make men and women sit still as we unfold the story of life… to make them take pen in hand to change a piece of paper into a precious document… to be sure that they will always be more glad than sorry. To acquire this capacity, we must have

1. *Knowledge* – precise understanding of the products we sell.
2. *Creative thinking* – awareness of the uses of our products. (Talk life before you talk life insurance.)
3. *The ability to motivate* – skills to persuade people to buy. (Understand high-touch as well as high-tech.)

We know that action without knowledge is fatal and that knowledge without action is futile. Life insurance that remains in the rate book is worthless. The only worthwhile life insurance is life insurance in force.

A book salesman was trying to sell a farmer a book entitled *How to Become a 50% Better Farmer.* Halfway through the presentation, the farmer interrupted and said, "Son, I am not buying that book. I am not doing half the things now that I know how to do."

Let not your learning exceed your deeds, lest you be like a tree with many branches and few roots. Many of us already have more sales ideas than we can ever use. What we need is to more intensively develop our personal resources – the ability to prospect, to make appointments, to effectively conduct the interview, and to develop the technique of the close. Remember, in many instances, the close starts with the approach. Your mannerism, personality, and sincerity must instill confidence in prospects so that they will say to themselves, "This is the life insurance agent I am ready to listen to."

7.

Work

One of the great stories that comes to us from the past is that of the man who one day stood beside Michelangelo, the master artist of all time, and asked him, as he gazed upon one of his great frescoes, to tell him the secret of his genius. Michelangelo, turning to him, said, "After 20 years of heartbreaking toil you ask me the secret of my genius. Genius, my friend, is work and an infinite capacity for taking pains."

Work nights, Sundays, and holidays to establish yourself, to reach your goal. As time goes on, you will find that you can program your own work schedule and that, for the most part, you can make appointments that suit *your* time frame.

Keep in mind that the only place where success comes before work is in the dictionary.

I don't want to give you the impression that I'm a workaholic. I never have been. I work until my work is done. I believe in working smart, not hard. I am not impressed with hard workers. I've attended industry meetings for years and have heard speakers brag about working 15 hours a day, that they haven't taken a vacation in years, and that they've developed an ulcer. Don't do that!

I have never come home in the evening and said, "Oh, what a hard day I've had!" I've never felt that way because I try to organize my time in such a way that I don't cripple myself emotionally or physically.

8.

Perseverance

U.S. President Calvin Coolidge once said, "Nothing in the world can take the place of perseverance. Talent will no; nothing is more common than unsuccessful men with talent. Genius will not; unrewarded genius is almost a proverb. Education will not; the world is full of educated derelicts. Perseverance and determination alone are omnipotent."

Persevere. But do not *persist*. To persevere and to persist mean to be constant, resolute, and steadfast. Only one, however, will gain us the admiration of our fellow man. The other will produce animosity.

Wherein lies the shading? Persevere is almost uniformly employed in the good and high sense of holding a worthy course, to continue despite discouragements. Persist often connotes an annoying or perverse adherence to a demand or purpose that may well be abandoned.

We *persevere* when we carefully and conscientiously prospect, make appointments, hold interviews, follow up, follow through, and refuse to become upset or discouraged.

We *persist* when we *insist*, as though we had a *right* to a prospect's time and a *right* to *demand* his or her business. If you are told to call back at another time, be it next week, next month, or next year, *persevere*. But if you are told "No," don't persist.

In short, to persist is to be a pest; to persevere is to be a professional. Dr. Samuel Johnson, the 18th Century English author, said, "Great works are performed not by strength, but by perseverance."

If I possess one character trait, it's perseverance. I can point to examples throughout my career where perseverance has paid off tremendously. If I call somebody and that person is not in, and I leave a message to call me back and I don't get a call, I don't give up. I persevere and continue to call. I persevere with people who say, "call back in two months"; I make a note and they hear from me in two months. Positive situations have often developed because of my perseverance.

As soon as a person says to me, "Lester, I don't mind seeing you and I don't mind if you call, but I'm not going to buy any insurance from you because my brother-in-law is in the insurance business," or "I have all the insurance I'm ever going to buy and it's not worth your while to call me again," or "I've given consideration to this, Lester, and I'm going to pass," then I no longer persevere. Pushing anything beyond this point is persistence and that would make me a pest. I persevere only until I receive a firm no or a reason to stop calling.

9.

Determination

Playwright George Bernard Shaw said, "People are always blaming their circumstances for what they are. I don't believe in circumstances. The people who get on in this world are the people who get up and look for the circumstances they want, and if they can't find them – make them."

Applause from President Gerald Ford and others as Mr. Rosen received the John Newton Russell Memorial Award at the Annual Convention of the National Association of Life Underwriters, Anaheim, California, 1975

    A man in trunks steps out on the railroad tracks, hitches a chain to the observation car, and pulls. The whole 72 tons of steel follow him along the track. He is 47 years old and his name is Angelo Siciliano.

    Angelo was raised in the slums of Brooklyn, the son of Italian immigrants. At age 16 he was a 97-pound runt, pale, nervous, and a prey to bullies. One Saturday Angelo went with some boys to a museum. He was transfixed by the statues of Apollo and Hercules.

That evening Angelo Siciliano clipped a series of bodybuilding exercises from a newspaper and began making himself over in the likeness of a Greek athlete.

He never gave up. He kept going when everyone sneered at his feeble display of muscle. He started inventing his own exercises, pitting one muscle against another, and gradually – there was no doubt about it – Angelo was beginning to bulge in all directions. He eventually became "the world's most perfectly developed man," possessor of the true classic physique – a blend of Hercules and Apollo.

Angelo Siciliano later became known to the world as Charles Atlas. He was not satisfied with his circumstance and he did something about it. He is now one of the most acclaimed bodybuilders of all time.

Many years ago at a Tennessee State Life Insurance Underwriters Sales Congress, I heard a thrilling address by Ray Busby, an officer of a life insurance company. I complimented Ray on his outstanding presentation, which was developed magnificently and presented forcefully without referring to a single note. Ray said, "Lester, this may be of interest to you. When I was a youngster, I stuttered so badly that I was not able to talk on the telephone. When I was older, I decided to do something about it. So I went to a speech and hearing school, after which I took public speaking lessons. The results are what you have heard today."

Ray Busby was not satisfied with his circumstance and he did something about it.

At a Million Dollar Round Table meeting in 1983, I introduced myself to a fellow member who told me his name was Paul Jeffers. We talked for several minutes about the excellence of the meeting and the outstanding presentations that were given by the main platform speakers. He said, "Lester, unfortunately I missed what some of the speakers had to say because when they turned their heads to the side I could not read their lips. You see, I am totally deaf." I was astonished. Here I was, carrying on a conversation with a deaf man who was responding as though he had heard every word. From that day on, Paul and I became close friends. His accomplishments are unbelievable – 14 consecutive years of life and qualifying membership in the Million Dollar Round Table, president of the Sacramento Life Underwriters Association, national membership chairman of NALU, president of the California Association of Life Underwriters, and California LUPAC chairman. Paul has spoken hundreds of times at various sales congresses and life underwriters association meetings in every state and Canadian province.

Paul Jeffers was not satisfied with his circumstance and he did something about it. He could not hear, but he learned to communicate by reading lips.

Act as though it were impossible to fail, and remember that *the only time you fail is the last time you try*.

Yesterday is gone forever. Don't brood over it. Mistakes are bound to occur. They are part of life, shots that are missed in golf, cases that are lost. A poem, for which I have lost the source, goes like this:

> *Prepare for tomorrow, and as you go through life,*
> *You may find that one path may fail, but there are more.*
> *And if it should be so that one is fruitless,*
> *Turn from it and another pathway go.*
> *Weep with a broken hope if weep you must, but not too long.*
> *A new trail seek – it waits for you, new hope within its song.*

10.

Leadership

Somewhere along the way I found these paragraphs.

> *President Abraham Lincoln's of war told him that a general had been captured and advised Lincoln to create a new general. Lincoln said, "I can promote a colonel and create a general, but I cannot create a leader. Leaders create themselves."*
>
> *Leadership! If you don't have it, you can't buy it! A law cannot be passed to give it to you. IT can't be assigned, transferred, or sold to your heirs. It is nonnegotiable. The mysterious acquisition of the qualities that cast you as a leader must be earned – and sometimes it is a long, painful process. In all areas of society we have seen those who have tried to buy leadership with their wealth – without success. Others have tried to acquire it by force – only to be broken in the attempt. History is replete with the failures of children who had hoped to inherit it from their parents.*
>
> *Leadership is more elusive than a dream and as easy to lose as your reputation. Probably not since the time of Moses has the need for leadership been so great as today, and there probably has not been a period in history when that statement has not been made.*

A leader is in control of the troops, in control of the business, in control of the situation. Consequently, if you are in control of a situation, you establish a rapport and you instill confidence in the person to whom you're speaking.

Conclusion

My father was born in 1871 in Poland and had perhaps two years of formal education. He was almost totally self-educated, yet I consider him one of the most intelligent men I've ever known. He left home at age 10 and went to Germany, then to England, and finally to the United States at age 17. He once told me, "Lester, I've never lost a dime that my father gave me because he never gave me anything!" He was an avid reader, and he loved music and the opera. He took elocution lessons. He became a very successful businessman and was president of his trade association.

My mother came to the United States in 1891 from Germany. She was very well educated. She spoke German, English, and French fluently. She gave the four of us (two boys and two girls) formal German lessons has children so we could converse in German.

We had mother and father who were bright, responsible hard workers, who led us on the righteous path, so that we grew up that way.

Mr. and Mrs. Lester and Pat Rosen

I've been blessed with a wonderful wife and children and a long and rewarding career. Why should I retire? I enjoy what I am doing. I look forward to every day – almost invariably, something unusual comes up. Man does not grow old by getting old; he only grows old by not growing.

For those of you who have read this treatise, I wish for you, as stated by the Paulist Fathers, ". . . continued growth and to let the highest achievement of today be just the *starting point* for tomorrow."

Index

15-minute break, 27

A

ability to pay premiums, 28
acknowledging favors, 31
action, 40
Aetna Life Insurance Company, xiv–xv
Ameritas Life Insurance Company, ix
answering communications promptly, 31
anticipate responses, 33
appointments, 25
assistant, 26
Atlas, Charles, 48
attitude, 39

B

build trust, 31
Busby, Ray, 48
business association, 28
business insurance field, 28

C

calendar, 26
calling prospects, 29
Chartered Life Underwriters, vi
circumstances, creating one's own, 47–48
cold calling, 29
Columbia University, 22
compassion, 35
confidence, 22, 34–35
confirm appointments, 25
conversation about life insurance, 23
Coolidge, Calvin, 45
courtesy, 31
criterion for prospecting, 28

D

depression, 39

E

Eliot, T.S., 33
empathy, 35
endless chain system, 28
executive leadership, 23
Executive Leadership Institute, 22–23
executive profiles, 28
exercise, 31

F

first appointment, 29
Ford Foundation, 22
Ford, Henry, 30
Frankfurter, Felix, 30
friends, 30
functional specialist, 30

G

genius, 43
goal setting, 21
going to lunch, 27

H

habits, 27
Hooks, Dr. Benjamin L., xi
How do you reach a prospect?, 35
Huebner Gold Medal, vi, x
Huebner, Dr. Solomon, viii–ix, xii, xv–xvii

J

Jeffers, Paul, 48
John Newton Russell Memorial Award, vi
Johnson, Dr. Samuel, 45

K

keep promises, 31
King, Carole, 28
Knight, Charles Bennett, ix
knowledge, 40

L

leaders create themselves, 51
leadership, 51
leading question, 27
learning, 40
Life Underwriter Training Council, vi
Lincoln, Abraham, 51
LinkedIn, 28
lists, 28

M

magic formula for success, 27
Maltz, Dr. Maxwell, 33
McCahan, Dr. David, viii, xii–xiv, xvi
MDRT Annual Meeting, vi
mediocrity, 21
Memphis Life Underwriter Association, vi
Michelangelo, 43
Million Dollar Round Table (MDRT), vi, ix, 48
misconceptions about prospects, 30
mobile delivery service, 26
money for future delivery, xvi

N

NAACP, xi
NALU, 48
National Association of Life Underwriters, vi
National Service Life Insurance, ix
National Underwriter, 28
new business firms, 28
new partnerships, 28
newspapers, 28
nobility, 21
number-of-cases goal, 21

O

organizing one's values, 37

P

Pennsylvania Bell Telephone, 22

perseverance, 46
persevere, 45
persist, 45
persistence, 46
personal resources, 41
pick-up service, 26
policy peddler, 35
preparation, 33
presentation, 22
priorities, 37
production goals, 21
prominent people, 30
prospecting intelligently every day, 28
prospects, 28
Psycho-Cybernetics, 33
public speaking, 22

Q

qualified prospects, 28

R

recession, 39
recipe for the attainment of success, 37
reliability, 31
respond promptly, 31
Rhodes College, 22
Rothkrug, Paul, 35
Russell, Dr. Hugh, 37

S

self improvement, 22
self-confidence, 23
selling in tough times, 39
setting goals, 21
Shaw, George Bernard, 47
Siciliano, Angelo, 47
single-deposit deferred annuities, 28
Socrates, 34
Southwestern College, 22
success, 27
superiority, 21

support person, 26

T

taking courses, 23
talking about life, xvi
talking about life insurance, 34
telephone script, 29
Tennessee State Association of Life Underwriters, vi
Tennessee State Life Insurance Underwriters Sales Congress, 48
The American College, ix, xvi
time, 25
Toastmasters Club, 22
trust, 35

U

Union Central Life Insurance Company, vi–vii, ix, xv
University of Pennsylvania, xii, 22

V

volume goal, 21

W

Whaley, Geneva, 26
Wharton School, xii, xvi
why people buy, 35
widows, 28–29
work ethic, 31
working smart, 43